A Fraction's Goal—
Parts of a Whole

A Fraction's Goal— Parts of a Whole

by Brian P. Cleary

illustrated by Brian Gable

M MILLBROOK PRESS / MINNEAPOLIS

Fractions are a portion,

a piece,

or just a part

of something that is larger,
like this segment on this chart.

Or look at this round pizza.
It can be cut in 2

or 4

or 6

or 8 or more—
whatever best suits you.

But let's say that it's cut in 2
and you pick up 1 slice.

If you've got 1 piece out of 2,
it's $\frac{1}{2}$ to be precise.

9

Next, cut that pizza into 4

and take 1 single piece.

10

That's $\frac{1}{4}$ now—can you see how the size has been decreased?

11

So now, if someone wants $\frac{1}{2}$, 2 slices will be needed.

$\frac{2}{4}$ and $\frac{1}{2}$ are the same; they're different ways to read it.

$\frac{7}{8}$ of jugglers,

and $\frac{1}{2}$ of the mayors.

Pretend you have 3 uncles and 2 came for a visit.

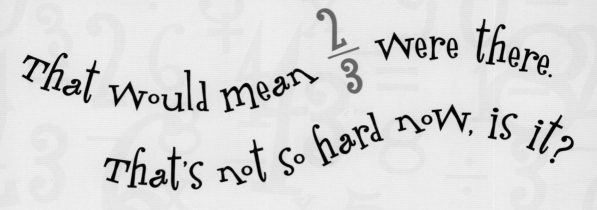

That would mean $\frac{2}{3}$ were there. That's not so hard now, is it?

Let's say the third one then showed up to join in all the fun.

That's 1 whole group of uncles,
'cause $\frac{3}{3}$ equals 1.

Fractions come in handy
if you ever help with baking.

You'll see them in the recipes

for breads and cakes you're making.

$\frac{3}{4}$ tablespoon of salt . . .

add $\frac{2}{3}$ cup of flour . . .

$\frac{2}{3}$ CUP

$\frac{5}{8}$ cup of chocolate chips . . . .

and bake for $\frac{1}{2}$ hour.

23

The numerator is the word for the number that's on top.

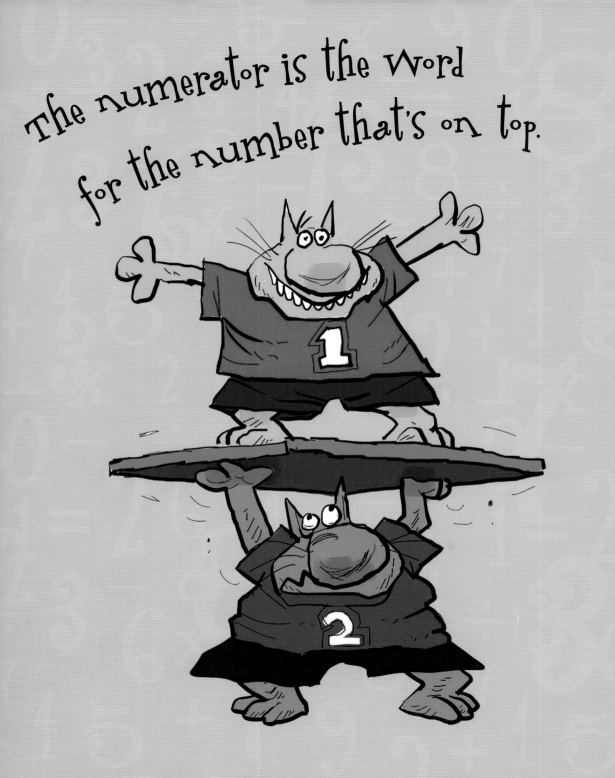

Like the 3 that's in, "We lost $\frac{3}{10}$ of this year's crop."

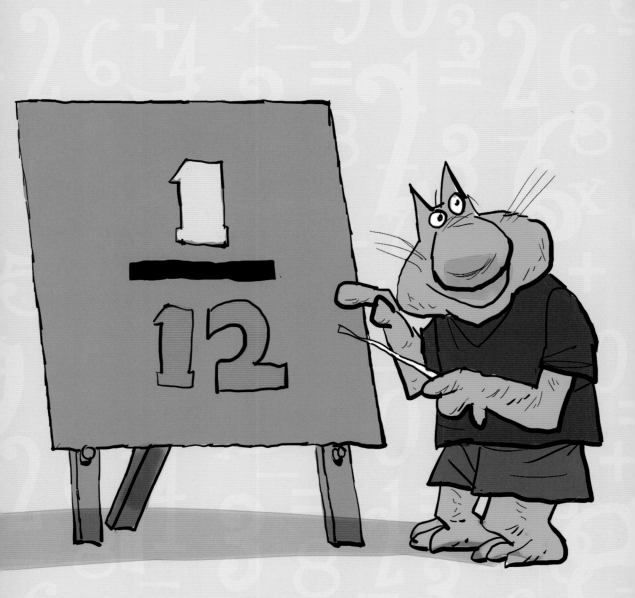

The number underneath the slash
is a denominator.

Note that nearly all the time
this bottom number's greater.

You'll know more than just a portion
if you give them half a chance!

So, what is a fraction?
Do you know?

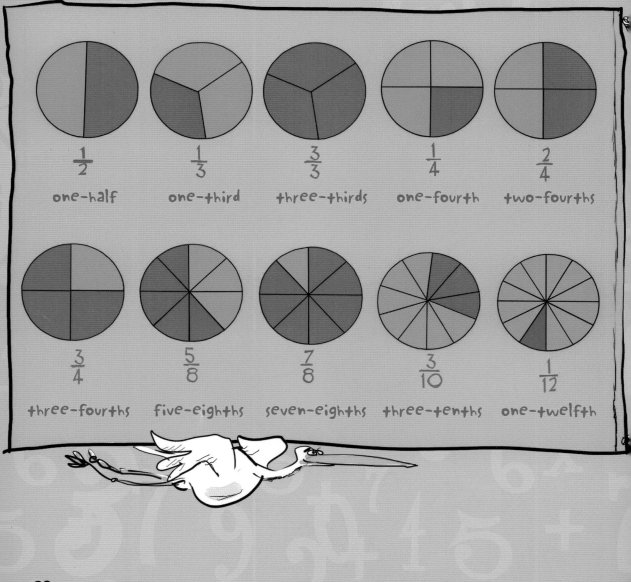

$\frac{1}{2}$	$\frac{1}{3}$	$\frac{3}{3}$	$\frac{1}{4}$	$\frac{2}{4}$
one-half	one-third	three-thirds	one-fourth	two-fourths

$\frac{3}{4}$	$\frac{5}{8}$	$\frac{7}{8}$	$\frac{3}{10}$	$\frac{1}{12}$
three-fourths	five-eighths	seven-eighths	three-tenths	one-twelfth

ABOUT THE AUTHOR & ILLUSTRATOR

Find activities, games, and more at www.brianpcleary.com

BRIAN P. CLEARY is the author of the best-selling Words Are Categorical© series as well as the Math Is Categorical©, Food Is CATegorical™, Adventures in Memory™, and Sounds Like Reading© series. He has also written Six Sheep Sip Thick Shakes: And Other Tricky Tongue Twisters, The Punctuation Station, and several other books. Mr. Cleary lives in Cleveland, Ohio.

BRIAN GABLE is the illustrator of many Words Are Categorical© books and the Math Is Categorical© series. Mr. Gable also works as a political cartoonist for the Globe and Mail newspaper in Toronto, Canada.

Millbrook Press
A division of Lerner Publishing Group, Inc.
241 First Avenue North
Minneapolis, MN 55401 U.S.A.

Website address: www.lernerbooks.com

Main body text set in RandumTEMP 35/48.
Typeface provided by House Industries.

Library of Congress Cataloging-in-Publication Data

Cleary, Brian P., 1959-
    A fraction's goal : parts of a whole / by Brian P. Cleary ; illustrated by Brian Gable.
       p.   cm. — (Math is CATegorical)
    ISBN: 978-0-8225-7881-9 (lib. bdg. : alk. paper)
    1. Fractions—Juvenile literature. 2. Ratio and proportion—Juvenile literature. I. Gable, Brian, 1949- ill. II. Title.
QA117.C54 2011
513.2'6—dc22   2010051518

Manufactured in the United States of America
1 — DP — 7/15/11